The [...] Journal

(Recherche de Perdu Journal Intime)

By Phillip Maguire

The Lost Journal
(Recherche de Perdu Journal Intime)

Kevin couldn't remember exactly where he lost it. It was sometime during his trips that day but he didn't know where. So he did what he always did when trying to find lost things: Where did I have it last? He recalled writing in it outside the Metropolitan Museum at Cleopatra's needle and afterwards at Strawberry Fields. Did he put it away after writing there? He wasn't sure. He had been so distracted by the crowd and the singing.

Once again a large crowd had gathered at the memorial for John Lennon's birthday, October 9th. As always, there was a group chant of Give Peace a Chance and some thin longhaired dude was playing acoustic guitar and singing "Imagine." The singer's red-rimmed eyes belied some substance. He felt as though he had seen him before. But since Kevin came every year, he assumed the dude had also been there.

For the past thirteen years Kevin took off work each year on John Lennon's birthday. He always did the same thing: rode the PATH train to Penn station, took the uptown subway to seventy-seventh street, walked to the Metropolitan Museum, visited the Egyptian collection on the first floor, and sat by Cleopatra's needle behind the museum before heading to Strawberry Fields. But this time he lost his journal.

Kevin had been keeping a journal on and off (mostly on, recently) since high school. In the beginning he wrote in it infrequently, usually a stray poem or idea but now he tried to write in it every day, even if it was just the day, date and time. Now he seldom missed a day's entry. He wrote poetry, flash-fiction and short stories. Kevin imagined himself a minor author. He had several pieces published online and in print. He had been paid for only two of these.

Still, Kevin enjoyed the self-expression he got from writing and he carried his journal everywhere. He always used the same Meade 6x9 inch, three-subject notebook. He liked the blue lined white pages and the pocket inside the front cover where he could keep important papers: work schedule, appointments, phone numbers, etc. The wide spiral binding offered a place to slide a pen inside and hook the end so that it was handy. The combination made a ready writing desk anywhere. He carried the notebook and pen combination in a drab olive-green, U.S. Army surplus, WWII canvas Field Bag. The bag also held whatever book he was currently reading. The bag, the book, the notebook/pen/journal went everywhere with Kevin.

Kevin didn't notice the journal was gone until the next day. When got home from his yearly trip he dumped the bag on the coffee table next to the computer. He intended to copy any meaningful pieces onto Word later. But the next day the bag was empty except for Joseph Conrad's "Heart Of Darkness." He searched the small apartment knowing all the time it wasn't there.

Kevin recalled writing something in the journal while sitting in the sun on a bench at the Central Park memorial while people sang "Strawberry Fields," off-key and too slow. He had written part of the lyrics that struck him as insightful:
" Living is easy with eyes closed
Misunderstanding all you see."

That's the last time he remembers seeing the journal.

 Finally he had to confront the fact that the journal (and how many month's writings?) was gone. He considered retracing his steps of the day before but he also knew that it would be fruitless. It was certainly gone now. So how did he lose the journal?

As best he could guess, he might have been too distracted at Strawberry Fields to replace it in the bag. Or did he take it out on the subway and forget to put it away? Kevin remembered the guy in the corner of the subway car, the one with the beard and he remembered the strange way he looked at Kevin. His eyes were exceedingly small, barely the size of dimes and closely spaced so they both seemed in the center of his narrow face. In fact, all his features: short mouth, thin nose and scant eyebrows crowded into the center. In many ways, he looked like Kevin. Did he get distracted by him, and leave it on the subway seat?

So, resigned, after work Kevin bought a new Meade notebook and Uniball pen. His first entry was:

Friday   10/9/12

A new day, another journal. I left the last one on the subway yesterday. I'll be more careful with this one.

The next one was:

Saturday   10/10/12

Brilliant leaf letters fall
From deciduous pages
Scraping and crabbing
Across cold concrete

This aging autumn
This fading fall
Is sliding backwards
Into winter

Wednesday   10/31/12

All Hallow's Eve

The auld guldwife's well-hoordit nits,
Are round and round divided,
And monie lads' and lasses' fates
Are there that night decided.
"Hallowe'en"
by Robert Burns

"Come on, Anna." Ben tugged at Anna's witch's cape. "We're gonna miss all the good stuff." The good stuff was full sized candy bars: Hershey bars with almonds, Baby Ruths, and Reese's Peanut Butter Cups. Ben knew that people who gave out whole candy bars only bought a few boxes and when they were gone, the porch lights would go out and the door bell rings and knocks would go unanswered.

This was the first year thirteen year-old Anna and her ten year-old brother Ben were trick-or-treating on their own. Their costumes were homemade as always: Anna's cape was cut from a black trash bag, her pointed hat made of poster board from the dollar store, and her broom was her mother's yellow one. Ben's ghost was the classic white sheet with eyes and nose cut out. His mother didn't want to cut out the mouth but Ben insisted. He complained he couldn't breathe, but really wanted to sample candy as he went. Halloween was his favorite holiday.

"Ok. Let's go." Anna picked up her broom and a pillowcase for candy. Ben folded his arms and sulked -- the pillow case was bigger than his brown grocery bag. Anna noticed, took Ben's bag and handed him the pillowcase. "It goes with your costume," she rationalized.

Together they went out the door into the already dark street. Black and white they walked into the night. An afternoon rain spiced the air with wet concrete, musty leaves and wood smoke. Gold, rust, and brown leaves littered the lawns and sidewalks. Beneath the streetlamps, shadows shifted slightly in the breeze and whispered their sad secrets.

The neighborhood was already thick with trick-or-treaters: hobos, goblins, vampires and princesses. Children's chatter and laughter colored the air above their heads. Anna walked patiently with Ben to each door. They coasted along: up one side of a street, down the other, around the corners and then repeated the process. Their bags grew heavy with candy and treats.

While they walked Anna told Ben: "I've read that Halloween is linked to the Celtic festival of Samhain which meant 'summer's end'. They believed the boundary between the world and the Otherworld grew thin on Samhain, allowing evil spirits to pass through so the Celts wore costumes to disguise themselves to avoid harm. Later Christian churches associated it with All Hallows Day and it became known as All Hallows Evening or 'Hallowe'en'. But whatever you call it, Halloween is a night of restless spirits." Ben listened distractedly as he unwrapped another Three Musketeer bar.

Anna was tired but Ben was still stoked with sugar and chocolate when they turned the corner onto Eldritch St. The sounds of other children had fallen away with the hours and now they were alone. A pale wan moon cast an irregular circle in the center of the cul-de-sac. "This is the last street, ok?" Anna's voice wavered with cold. "Ok," Ben agreed.

They walked the uneven sidewalk beside the thick, gnarled trunks of aged trees. The air grew cold; their warm breath fogged. Amongst the trees there was a beating, as of wings. And low, labored breathing began somewhere in the dark above their heads. A sudden swirl of wind blew a helix of leaves into the air. There was an exhale of a putrid scent as some unseen, icy thing-something more an emptiness from a gash in the material world-grabbed Ben by the throat and snatched him up into the trees.

"Ben! Ben! Ben!" Anna shouted as she turned around, and around, and around. A white sheet wafted to the ground. Ben was gone.

Saturday   11/2/12

He taxied his worries
Upon his back
Shouldering misery in
Trunks of solitude

And so it was, autumn quickly changed to winter, and fall's brocaded and tapestried mountainsides became sere tans and browns of the dark months.

Kevin forgot the lost journal and its contents until one night he noticed an online poetry post. It was a poorly revised poem that was in Kevin's missing notebook. Mark Wayne was the fictionalized author. When Kevin notified the poetry site that the poem was one of his own, he was met with disbelief and disinterest. Since it was not a juried site, they gave him no satisfaction and declined to offer any information about the supposed author. Kevin chalked it up to imitation being the sincerest form of flattery.

Meanwhile Kevin continued with his entries in the new journal:

Saturday   11/9/12

Finger points
Wind ripples
Water moon

Sunday   11/10/12

Listening to roaring silence
Buzzing bees descend
From ceiling trees

Monday   11/11/12

There are times when all our worries
Evaporate like dew
There are times when all our sorrow
Just cannot make us blue
There are times when all our dreams and hopes
Dissolve without a clue

Tuesday   11/12/12

Rearranging words
Like furniture in a room
Sentences like
Rooms in a house

Wednesday   11/13/12

Fog lies low on flaxen fields

Book to get: Word Origins by John Ayto

Again Kevin had almost forgotten about his lost journal until he noticed one of his flash fiction pieces posted on another online literary site. This time the author was someone calling himself "WritYurLif." Once more, Kevin's inquiries went without response. He complained that he was the real author but since he had no proof there was no retraction. The site had a policy of anonimity so he couldn't find out who the thief was. However, Kevin was pleased that the piece received several positive comments.

Meanwhile, he continued to write in his new journal:

Saturday   *11/17/12*

<u>Going Solo</u>
The late leaves of autumn, scraps of chestnut, ocher and burnt sienna, littered the lawns of the homes they passed.

"I can't believe I'm going to Cedar Woods by myself."

"You're not going by yourself, Mom. I'm taking you."

"You know what I meant, Anna Marie."
"I know what you meant. (And I hate when you call me that.)

An awkward silence swelled between them. Sunlight slashed between almost leafless trees flashing the windshield making it blink off and on irregularly.

She lifted her chin slightly, looked out the side window at the fading day and said, "Your father always loved this time of year."

"I know, Mom." He's dead, Mom. We have to get on with our lives.
The road tapered and descended into the shadow of a mountainside still tapestried in fall's gaudy colors.

"I still can't believe I'm going to Cedar Woods by myself."

Monday   11/19/12

Karma Repair Kit: Items 1-4

1. Get enough food to eat, and eat it.
2. Find a place to sleep where it is quiet, and sleep there.

3. Reduce intellectual and emotional
   noise until you arrive at the silence
   of yourself, and listen to it.
4.

By Richard Brautigan

Tuesday   11/20/12

She loved everyone she fucked
And fucked everyone she loved

Wednesday   11/21/12

Moonlight whispers
White lace curtains

Friday   11/23/12

After the Deluge

Ben ran like the others working in the
fields when the wall of water rushed
towards them. The levee was breached.
When he stumbled and fell, the water
caught him and tumbled him amongst its
debris of vegetation, limbs and lumber. A
sharp blow on the side of his head made
him dazed and helpless. Something flat

smacked his chest and, like a hand, lifted him to the roiling surface. Clinging to that wooden pallet, Ben vacillated from fear to hope. A world of wet surrounded him: swirling waters beneath and a deluge from above.

He never learned to swim so the water took him where the limited square of boards went. A long time passed before this raft bumped amongst the tangled branches of a partly submerged Hickory tree. Anxious to be rid of the water's whim, he clambered onto the shag-barked lower limbs and rested in a crook between branches, well above the water.

Dark days and nights blended until the rains relented. On the fifth day the torrent ended. A weak pale sun emerged and he saw how the flood waters spread outward from the river making all the visible miles of flat fields a muddy chocolate. Where there were once rows of cotton and corn, there was now brown all around except for the few green trees whose branches broke the surface. Ben was stranded in the branches of one of those trees.

After the rain, stillness came. The surging waters began to settle. The air was filled with silence except for the rare caw, caw, caw of a crow. Soon a heavy sun sweated a soiled stench from the soup of decay around the small green island; Ben was marooned in a swamp of fetid odors.

Hunger made him try the tree's unripe fruit. The leathery green flesh was hard to remove even when scraped against the coarse bark. The nut's shell was tough as well: squeezing between the palms didn't work, smashing two together only hurt his hands, a smack from a shoe shot one into a distance. But when he crammed one between two bark ridges and stomped on it with the heel of his shoe, it shattered into fragments of nutmeat and shell. The meat was sharp and bitter but edible.

Although surrounded by water, Ben was thirsty. He could not drink from the stinking soup. Instead he licked the wet leaves and lapped from wells in the bark. After the harshest pangs of hunger and

thirst abated, he rested in his crook and
hummed a boyhood hymn. Then he began
to sing it softly:

"...
You gotta move,
you gotta move,
But when the Lord gets ready,
You gotta move.

You may be high.
You may be low,
You may rich,
A-ha, a-ha...
You may be poor,
But when the Lord gets ready,
You gotta move."

Surrender was Ben's last sacrament.

Saturday   11/24/12

Casting a cognitive net
To catch an ineffable reality -
Experience without words
Knowing beyond thinking

Wednesday   11/28/12

Out of the shadows
Beyond the night lake
Ghostly trees' bony bright branches
Shimmer through the mist

Saturday   12/1/12

Why Windows?

Why do windows
Make us wonder
I wonder

We gaze from them
At moon
At stars
At the backyard breeze

We stare at
Sea and sand
The blue on blue horizon
Scrolling slowly to the shore

We look at famous skylines:
Empire State buildings
Eiffel towers
Coliseums
Big Bens
The Space Needle

We watch the
Scudding shadows
Of passing clouds
Cross the mountains and meadows

We look
We see
We wonder

Why?
I wonder

Tuesday   12/5/12

<u>Bunny Ears</u>

Anna and her sister played with the baby
bunnies. LeeAnne had found the nest in
the long grass just beyond the garden. The
three bunnies were small, the biggest still
fit inside their small hands, but their
gray fur was full and smooth to the touch.
Their small brown eyes were alert and
their noses twitched with exploration.

Anna stroked the biggest one's long,
smooth, soft ears between her thumb and
index finger. She smiled as she traced its
inverted "U" with her finger and looked
at the pinkish-buff of its interior and the
latticework of red blood vessels. She felt
her own cold, coarse, cartilaginous,

crescent ears and frowned. She wished she had soft bunny ears.

"Anna, LeeAnne, it's bedtime," their mother called.

In the morning LeeAnne shook Anna awake. "Anna something's happened to the bunny. Its ears…" LeeAnne halted when she saw the bunny ears, now pale, with bloody roots, on the pillow beside her sister's head.

Tuesday   12/14/12

She wore a band
Of flowers in her eyes
That candied the air
With sunshine colors as
Fragrant moments radiated
From her fine fingers
That lingered like noon

Sunday   12/19/12

December Failings

While night throbbed
Confusion wove a
Tattered shawl for
My sad shoulders as
Some lonely sorrow
Sifted down from the
Dark December sky

From under the
Leaves of night
Silence seeped deep
Between unsaid
Unheard words
And within the
Walls of wind
Failings fluttered
Unfettered

Kevin dreamed about the man on the subway, his
beard, his small features, how he looked like him, and
the strange way he looked at Kevin. He dreamt the
man picked the journal up from the subway seat and
was reading it and laughing. He awoke feeling
confused; the dream seemed so real.

Months passed. Fall faded to winter. Snow fell. The winter holidays passed and a New Year started.

Monday   1/1/13

Another year

Living in the attic of discontent
Where wishes, wants and worries
Scurry across the dusty floor
With pricking sticks of unhappiness
I dislike the canto of this Lila.
Tuesday   1/2/13

"Sometimes you have to lay down the unanswerable questions."

Wednesday   1/3/13

The Smells of Silence
Musty basement
Damp dirt
Mildewed books
Coffee
Stink of cigarette smoke
Saltsweet sea breeze
Hint of Shalimar

Freshly cut grass
Wood fire
Leaf smoke

Saturday   1/5/13

He hates the clear cold
That stings the nose
Burns his lungs and
Numbs his ears
The clear cold that
Bone aches
Cold bright light
Pains the eye

Monday   1/8/13

Sitting quietly
Unwinding the knot
Of thinking
Remembering less
Forgetting more
Waiting in the
Inconsistent solitude
Of memory

Thursday   1/10/13

Mom's and Rod Stewart's birthdays. Mom would have been ninety now.

Of course Kevin's actual entries were more frequent than this, and more chaotic with revisions, cross outs, mention of minor incidents of life and personal notes. These are only excerpts, cleaned up representations of his notes.

Wednesday   1/16/13

Birth is a slow death

Tuesday   2/5/13

I can't believe it. Someone has posted my flash-fiction story, Night Flight, online:

Ben fought through the thicket. Brambles and thorns tore at his naked flesh. Sewage stench sweated from his shit-stained body. Behind him the tracking dogs barked in eager pursuit. He crawled through the last dense brush then sprinted the clearing and made a leap for the prison fence.

Ben's convulsing body thudded to the ground beneath the sign: __Danger: High Voltage__

This time the author was luv2writ. But again the site on which the flash-fiction was posted had no interest in Kevin's claim of authorship and would not divulge information about luv2writ.

Upset by the plagarism, Kevin decided to see if it had been found on a subway car. But attempts to call the MTA lost and found only resulted in a telephone tree that didn't allow talking to a person. So he went to the lost and found department on the lower mezzanine of Penn Station.

It took a short time to find the record of the journal. It had been found and sent to the lost and found department the same day Kevin lost it. But someone representing himself as Kevin had claimed it the same day. He had signed for it under Kevin's name. The imposter also left an address when he signed for the journal: but it was Kevin's address – and phone number. Kevin decided he must have left something in the front folder with his information on it.
He left the department totally confused and frustrated. Who was this imposter? How could he find him? Why was he doing this?

Wednesday   2/13/13

Winter-stormed trees wear
Crystalline hair while
Ice fractal flowers
Blossom on windows
As February
Falls lightly, whitely

Friday   2/15/13

I looked in a mirror
And looking back at me
Was looking back at me

Sunday   2/17/13

Perhaps I'll send
My poems to SETI
To disperse my verse
Across the universe

Friday   2/22/13

Focus on the
Nexus of now
The unfolding Tao

Wednesday   2/27/13

Apophis (2004MN4)

"Honey, did you see this?" Ben asks as he folds the newspaper, rustling the burnt toast and coffee scented air. Then he runs his thin age-spotted hand along a crease as he lays it upon the breakfast table and clears his throat in preparation to read aloud:
"NASA announced today that there is an outside chance that Apophis, a stadium sized, stony asteroid could strike the Earth in 2036 with the force of 100,000 times the blast over Hiroshima.

"So," Anna says with her detached distain as she sips her coffee, "you'll be 109 and I'll be 107. We'll be dead. So who cares?"

At that moment, Twenty million miles from Earth, its rocky surface dimly reflecting the distant sun, Apophis (named after the ancient Egyptian enemy of Ra, Apep, the Un-creator) tumbles slowly as it races into a gravitational

"keyhole" which locks it into a
catastrophic collision course with Earth.

Thursday   2/28/13

Dark ducks line
Orthodox Ogham along
The iced streambed
Frothy fog forms
Over frozen river

Friday   3/1/13

A Fine Line
Ben followed the fine line of a crack in
the green plaster above the gray metal file
cabinet. It meandered down the wall like
a rural highway on a map, snaking and
curving through unseen lands, climbing
over ridges, rushing down valleys, past
farms and small towns, beside train
tracks, over bridges and through tunnels
before intersecting with a series of
circular cracks that looked like beltways
surrounding a city.

A black triangular hole sat at their
center, as if something had been thrown

or struck there. Busted lath slats projected from the hole's sides like broken ribs coated in crumbling grey plaster flesh.

Some fragment of Ben's attention knew She was talking again. She was pleading her case, again. She was telling the therapist what an abusive, alcoholic, asshole he was-again.

Ben stared into the death in the center of that triangular black hole and imagined her face bloodied and bruised, her now quiet mouth contorted in some silent cry.

Just wait, Ben Thought. Just wait.

Saturday   3/2/13

I received a copy of "New Poetics" in the mail today. It published my poem "Change Of Seasons." But I never submitted it to them. In fact I never submitted it to any journal. I had just finished it when my journal was lost. Someone submitted it under my name too. Who is doing this? And why?

Monday   3/4/13

I called "New Poetics" today and
explained the circumstances. They asked
if I was the author, and I said yes. They
said the poem was submitted under my
name and had my address for a
complimentary copy of the issue.
I tried to explain that I hadn't submitted
it but they seemed doubtful. Who else
would have submitted it? They asked. I
said that I didn't know. They couldn't
provide any further information so I
ended the call.

Monday   3/11/13

Liberation

Ryan Mitchell saw it coming: Brian
Dawson smiled, flipped down his night
goggles and pointed his weapon at him. A
sizzling poker of pain burst above Ryan's
left eye; then a loosening, a lessening, a
falling away, dreamlike memories
floating down like leaves.

Life is a fatal illness; death is our true

essence, an unfettered spirit, without attachment, longing, or worry.

The Funeral

"I can't believe he's gone," Rachel wept. Her mother gently squeezed her slender wrist beneath the black linen cuff as three rifle shots fired. Rachel watched through tears when the flag was folded and the union tucked.

"This flag is presented on behalf of a grateful nation, ..." First Lieutenant Dawson said before handing her the folded flag. Mist shrouded the bugler's "Taps."

The Other Rachel

"Oh God, that feels sooo good," Brian Dawson cooed. Dark curls of hair fell backwards onto her arched back. Fendi, sweat and sex stained the sheets.

Rachel's crumpled and creased dark linen suit lay beside his dress blue uniform with its colored ribbons and marksmanship badges.

Friday   3/15/13

"Beware the ides of March"

Saturday   3/16/13

Patty's birthday. I need to call Allen.
Monday   3/18/13

Over and Out

"McMurdo, this is Shackleford. Over."

Silence.

"McMurdo, this is Shackleford. I'm in a snow cave ten miles east, waiting out the storm. I've marked the site with skis. Do you copy? Over."
Kevin Shackleford rests his head against the sled and closes his eyes. Time slides into unconscious awareness.

He stands beside the Elks' Club watching the high school band perform "Stars and

Stripes Forever." Scents of wet concrete and citronella wash through baby-handed trees. A girl sketches the air with a sparkler.

Kevin awakes to darkness. His wrists are wrought-iron, his fingers tongs. He tries the radio again: "McMurdo, this is Shackleford." Kevin pauses. "Over, and, out." Cold seduces time again.

He jumps from rock to rock on a jetty; waves swish and swash, hurling spray and smells of dried squid, barnacles, and brine. Kevin's father and Uncle Joe shout and laugh in drenched delight. Sunlight soaks, thaws, eases his breathing and lightens his limbs.

So this is what it's like to die. No fast forward film, only scenes in full bloom like a dream.

When the rescue team finds Shackleford, the radio is frozen in his hand; the dogs form an icy rosary around him.

Wednesday   3/20/13

I had a bizarre dream last night about
that strange bearded guy on the subway.
He was reading my journal and
laughing. Then he started to put it on a
computer. I woke up with a déjà vu
feeling.

Thursday   3/28/13

Slowly the wall began to change from a
smooth plane of blank beige to an
undulating landscape of tormented faces,
their mouths distended and distorted in
horrific howls of pain and suffering.
Saturday   3/30/13

Time is pluripotent: moments do not exist
until they crystallize from
a superposition of possibilities
then fate and freewill
intersect in the instant.

Monday   4/1/13

Another day, another week, another
month.

Wednesday   4/3/13

Something's wrong with the sun
They say
There's nowhere you can run
They say
Something's wrong with the sun
They say
Only eight minutes away
They say
Something's wrong with the sun
And there's nowhere to run

Tuesday   4/9/13

She loved everyone she fucked
And then fucked everyone she loved

Saturday   4/13/13

Trip to Eldritch

Some noxious smell, or sound, or thing,
made Ben fall up from his dream of soft
snow. He awoke with a jagged jolt and
tossed the comforter aside. A swirling
dizziness briefly whirled inside his head
when he sat up on the side of the bed. He

stared vacantly at the bedside clock watching the digital seconds blink between the numbers of 02:38. Ben was startled when the clock buzzed loudly and unexpectedly. He pushed the off button, but the alarm buzzed louder and more shrilly for many seconds; then it stopped and silence swarmed the darkness.

The light above the bed came on and brightened in steps. Ben rushed to the switch and turned it off; but the bulb brightened more. And when he flipped the switch to on, the light went off.

Then, without warning, the television set on the bureau came on by itself. Burgess Meredith sat on a library's ruined steps, raised his shattered eyeglasses and said: "That's not fair. That's not fair at all. There was time now. There was all the time I needed... It's not fair!"

When Ben switched the set off, the actor turned, looked directly at Ben and repeated: "That's not fair. That's not fair at all." before the picture winked out.

Next, the cell phone on the bedside table sounded ring tones while still off. Ben answered it and a soft voice asked "Are you ready?"

"Am I ready? Am I ready for what? Who is this?" Ben demanded, looking at the lightless phone. There was no answer.

The clock's radio came on; the clock was still blinking 02:38 as distorted music surged and wavered with the words:
   "Living is easy with eyes closed, misunderstanding all you see.
   It's getting hard to be someone but it all works out, it doesn't matter much to me. Let me take you down, 'cause I'm going to..."

Ben pulled the radio's plug from the outlet. The sudden silence shocked him. His ears pulsated. He stared at the clock that still blinked stalled time.

Then Ben's eyes were drawn to a corner by a preternatural darkness. The moon's gauzed light seemed to whisper something sinister in the shadows. He knelt in the corner where the faded gray rug lost its edge in the shadow. There was something almost visible in the depth of the corner. Ben edged his hand slowly forward. It penetrated unimaginably deep into the blackness.

His hand began to tingle. Not like the pins-n-needles when a hand's asleep, but as though little electrical sprites were dancing in his palm. Ben withdrew his hand and was surprised to find nothing there. He returned it to the shadow and the feeling returned; only now it had a pattern. It started in the center of his palm and slowly radiated out and down his fingers to their tips. It wasn't painful; it was mildly pleasant. It began to increase in intensity and the speed with which it spread to his fingertips. It felt warm and pulsating.

When Ben tried to pull his hand out to look at it again, he couldn't. It was strangely stuck. It wasn't caught as if in a trap or wedged in a space. It wasn't being tugged as if being pulled. He could move all his fingers, turn his hand over, and even bend it at the wrist. He just couldn't withdraw it.

Fear swept over Ben. He pulled hard; there was no movement. He swung his legs around and braced against the walls and used his leg muscles to pull. Still nothing. Sweating, Ben slumped to his side. That's when it happened: The darkness dilated; the blackness yawned into a gaping maw and swallowed Ben noiselessly.

Sunday   4/21/13

Bird-foot

Smoke rose from the center of the Great Kiva at Chetro Ketl. The air was spicy-sweet with the smell of the burning pinion pine. Bird-foot could hear the burbling voices of the men already seated inside.

They have not yet begun to sing, He thought.

An indigo night sky still clung to the west

of the pueblo buildings clustered in the canyon. A white wafer moon seemed to rest upon the western wall. The turquoise morning sky was streaked with gold and orange clouds above the mesa to the east. A coyote silhouette barked and yodeled. The summer solstice sun was about to rise. When its first rays formed a bright sepia rectangle on the dark west wall inside the kiva, illuminating the Kachina-priest, the men would start to sing "The Song of Ancestors."

I must hurry, Bird-foot thought, trying to quicken his limping pace, hobbled by the deformed left foot that was his namesake. It scribbled short sentences in the cinnamon dirt as he hurried.

I cannot be late. Father will not make a place for me. He will look away when I enter. I hope the others will not laugh at me again, Bird-foot thought.

Sunday   4/28/13

Poetic Injustice
The warm breeze was a smile
With the smell of damp earth
After the tin tasting rain
Water rushed white down a brook
And rainbows arched through clouds
With hard painful fingers
Singing the warmth of wind
As mountains wished happiness to the
clouds
Red rain arose from oatmeal fields
But rain can't rise it falls
Or perhaps it can do both
Or just a mumpsimus
If rust made steel rain
Birth is a slow death
Within the solitary book of faith
When her hazel eyes saw Ben
Ben swam though the air
He was Goliath
Holding the heavy feather
Life is full of no things
It will be forever now
De perdu temps

Wednesday   5/1/13

Time wore away the surface
And the substance of my love
Until only shadows lingered

You are a distant cloud
Colored in sunset
Fading, receding into night

Friday   5/3/13

Fill the moments of the day
With sensations, conceptualizations,
Nonsense and incense
Drain from the moments of the day
Vexations, intolerance, anger, fear
Envy and dislike
Add to the moments of the day
Joy, wonder and kindness

Wednesday   5/15/13

Moments scatter like
Ophelia's flowers

Monday   5/20/13

Still Waiting

I didn't expect to see her at the gallery
opening. We were never lovers. I didn't
have the nerve or the words to say. With
her husband she was all stripes, black and
white, the strong suit to his practiced
passive; to me she was unresolved,
unfocused, a blur.

"Hello, Elaine," I said to her hazel eyes.

"Hi, Ben, it's been a l-o-n-g time…" she
purred, over social conversations and the
obnoxious ringtone of some un-seen cell
phone.

She lingered on the "long"; her words
honeyed my heart. Her J'Adore lifted me
by both elbows. My blood bubbled.

"I've been working a lot." I lied.

"I hope you haven't been working too
hard…" her eyes smiled with the double
entendre. Her lips pursed just slightly.

With him, she was all declarative sentences, with me she was complex ones with subordinate clauses and ending in ellipses.

"Ben, I've been thinking…" her lips parted and some sentence started.

"Elaine. Elaine!" Her husband called across turning heads.

"Excuse me…" she touched my wrist and went. J' Adore lowered me.

My heart kissed her lips goodbye and I left.

Thursday   5/23/13

Ocean child
Ocean child
Never ripened
Stolen secrets
Sun turns
Cloud burns
World weeps
Rain rises
Ocean child

Ocean child

Sunday   6/2/13

I breathed out
As trees inhaled
Their roots swelling
Bosom Earth
Heaved and fell
Breathing me
Fold into the breathing
Fold into the void
The vast expanse of divinity
Infinity in a finite space
A broken bracket of words
Unsupported truth
Transparent thoughts
See-through ideas
Beyond words
Beyond concepts
Beyond beyond
In the notnow
In the nontime
In the nowhen

Tuesday   6/4/13

Thick lipped, thin hipped women
That think naughty is nice

Friday   6/10/13

The day stretched before me like a heated
plane: moments wavering and quaking
with possibilities.

Sunday   6/16/13

Young girls weave the air with hands
Their Chiclet smiles
Their early breasts
Soft moons

Saturday   6/22/13

Sitting in this lonely chair
Remembering how her hair
Would fall in golden curls
Over this wearied world

Monday   7/1/13

Cloud shadows swept
Her smile away
While dementia
Washed away her worries

Friday   7/5/13

Stretching the fabric of truth Until it tears

Friday   8/2/13

Trying to hold emptiness (in my mind).

Sunday   8/11/13

While night throbbed
Confusion knitted a
Tattered shawl for
My sad shoulders
Tuesday   8/13/13

The trees weep and wring their hands
The sea pounds upon the land
I wish she were here with me
To share this mystery

Tuesday   8/20/13

A lazy rain strayed
Across the lawn
And Seurated the pavement
Like a pointillist painting
Wednesday   8/28/13

The Fever

I swung the axe again and again and again. The first blow struck her outstretched arm above the elbow, leaving it dangle: a bleeding, broken bough. The next one split her collarbone, wedging shards into her chest. There was a sick sucking sound when I jerked the axe loose. The third strike cleaved her face from above her ear through her eye and nose and into her mouth. She gave a ghastly gasp then snorted and coughed a spray of blood as she stumbled backwards, falling onto the mauled and mangled manikins of her mother and brother marinating in an expanding pond of thickening red.

As I realized what I had done I began to weep uncontrollably. "I killed my whole family. I killed them all," I sobbed. I was still sobbing when I awoke from the dream. I began to get out of bed but I found my hands were tacky and stuck to the sheets. That's when I saw the blood on my hands. "Oh, God, no," I roared. When I awoke fully, I found my fevered body had sweated itself to the sheets; my hands were sticky with sweat. My wife and son and daughter smiled from the bedside; they knew the delirium had passed and I would recover from the fever.

Monday   9/1/13

I found a flyer for a poetry reading at "The Irish Pub" inside my door. Apparently it was slipped under the door during the night. The reading was last week.

Tuesday   9/2/13

I went to "The Irish Pub" and asked about the reading. The owner said that there had been several readers. I asked him to describe them. There had been four women and three men. One of the men was an older man with long white hair in a ponytail. Another was younger with small features and a beard. When I asked him if he could describe him better, the owner said he looked like me, with a narrow face and very small eyes, but he had a beard. When I asked if he remembered what he read, he could only recall that it was a prose poem or flash-fiction and that the man read from a spiral-bound journal. He had no other information, no way of getting in touch with him. But as I was leaving he said that, except for the beard, the man could have been my twin. Bewildered, I left the pub.

WHAT THE FUCK? I never read. I'm just too nervous to stand in front of an audience and read. I tried it once and it didn't go well. Who the hell is doing this?

I have no brothers, I have no sisters, and I have no twin. The owner described the man on the subway, the man I dreamed about. How is this happening?

There's another reading next week. I'm going to see if the prick shows up.

Friday   9/5/13

The Panty Drawer

She couldn't help herself. She just had to see. While Lynn was in the shower, she snuck into the bedroom. Knowing Lynn's personality she should have expected the eclectic assortment of furniture: the Louis Philipe cherry make-up vanity was covered with Dior and Elizabeth Arden cosmetics. A iron nineteenth century campaign canopy bed was made with steel gray duvet and white silk sheets. A rosewood Kobe lingerie dresser stood between windows dressed with a Japanese floral pattern.

They weren't in the top drawer, nor the second. The third drawer was the panty drawer. Inside a patchouli and musk sachet scented a cache of colors and styles: high-leg briefs, hip-huggers, bikinis, cheekies and thongs. There were garter belts too. She was mesmerized by the quantity and variety of panties. They were soft, warm cotton and cool, smooth silk. Black and blue, pink and purple, striped, polka- dots and lace trimmed. She was admiring a sexy red lace trimmed black bikini when Lynn walked in, a towel wrapped around his waist. "Mo-o-m," he said. "That's my private drawer."

"Yes. I know," she said placing the panty back and closing the drawer.

Thursday   9/11/13

I went back to "The Irish Pub" last night. There were seven readers, but he wasn't there. Some readings were ok and others were crap. Two of the four women were young girls who read rhyming love poems. The old guy with the white ponytail read some introspective drivel. One young man read a hip-hop, rap-like thing that was too difficult to follow. I asked each of them if they knew the guy with the beard. No one knew him, but he looked like me with a beard.

I'll keep going back until I find him.

Wednesday   9/17/13

I found a book upon the stair
There wasn't anyone anywhere
I opened it to take a look
It wasn't like any other book
The words were backwards
And ran together

Incomplete sentences
Ran on forever

Saturday   9/27/13

Evolution Redux

No one will ever know how The Great
Change happened. Before the end,
humanity sequenced the genome of
thousands of organisms as diverse as
amoebas, bacteria and humans. This
included transposons, or "jumping genes",
like: Harbinger_3 DR, Sleeping Beauty
and piggyBac, which could cut and paste
themselves into different genome
locations.
This information, once coded in GCAT
base pairs, had been translated into
binary code and stored on silicon
computer chips.

Perhaps it was the electromagnetic pulses
of Man's weapons during the war of the
Apocalypse that allowed the switching
and the mixing of those now binary
genes.

An oozing mass of primitive intelligence, millions of bits of RAM in a silicone sac, searches amidst the wreckage, scavenging for silicon, energy, and knowledge. The low, slow hum of its breathing is the only sound in this world of devastation and death. The edge of a faintly glowing screen attracts its attention.

A thin, slick, blue-green, pseudopod slides silently across the rubble. A slender projection slips between the ragged remains of twisted, tangled metal and tumbled concrete. It swarms across an ash-coated key. "You've got mail," a cheerful voice announces weakly.

Sunday   10/4/13

Lying in the naked
Yellow of noon

Monday   10/5/13

Poetry is without paraphrase

Tuesday   10/6/13

The Shadows (Just fr fun)

The shadows merged and melted then
fused into a semi-opaque pyroclastic
enamel that goffered and riffled in an
incandescent seiche, a vaporous heat
marcel, a fata morgana fluting above the
torridity of sand hammered by tireless
torrents of molten solar thunderbolts
roaring and crashing from limitless
vertical heights through vacant spaces
without meaning or purpose until night's
dark ocean washed away the residual
califacient radiation and swallowed all
shadows from this canicular day, leaving
only one unanswered burning question:
Is causality simply a syllogism of time?

Saturday   10/10/13

October Twilight

With the day's last light
The low western clouds glow gold
In the blue clear cold

Tuesday   10/13/13

Lost and Found

Ben Watson's casket hung above an oblong of space surrounded by a multicolored mosaic of fallen leaves. Less than a finger-count of people made an oval of onlookers. A sharp, sweet, yet spicy smell rose from the musting ground. The sky fell in droplets all around.
After Father Flaherty gave his grave-side homily, a short, balding man with a fringe of monk's gray and melted facial features spoke:

"Lieutenant Ben Watson was my platoon leader in Korea. He saved my life. He pulled me from a burning foxhole. His hands and arms were severely burned. For this he was awarded the Purple Heart. His final request was that "Amazing Grace" be played at his funeral. I am here to honor that request." He pushed the button on a small tape recorder and Johnny Cash's a cappella steel and tempered glass voice sang:

Amazing grace, how sweet a sound,
That saved a wretch like me.
I once was lost but now am found.
Was blind, but now, I see

A leaf fell slowly from the sky--a single
tear from a single eye.

Monday   10/15/13

Haiku Inyerruptus

October trees wear
[Short chevron of geese flies south]
Crinkled autumn air

Tuesday   10/16/13

A sunrise sky
Of fruit and flower
Peach and rose

Wednesday   10/14/13

Struggle to live
Then slowly die

Thursday   10/15/13

My thinking is like
The strings of gale-tossed wind chimes:
Tangled and knotted

Saturday   10/17/13

Excess Baggage

"We're still losing altitude." Kendai
Bahouti shouted, wrestling for control of
the twin-engine aircraft. Large beads of
sweat coalesced on his brow, ran down his
nose and dripped in expanding dark
discs on his tan shirt.

The anthropology team was en route from
Nairobi to the new Turkana Basin
Institute in the Rift Valley province of
Kenya. Their flight took them over small
fumaroles and steam vents from forest
covered calderas.

But during the low level traverse of Lake
Turkana, a wall of flamingos lofted into

the air, their heavy pink bodies slammed into the plane, spidered the windshield and bent the four left propeller blades so that they looked like a wilted blood stained flower.

"Toss out anything you can." Kendai ordered. Then began a drizzle of equipment, luggage, and computers drooled over several miles of coffee, wheat, barley, and bean fields.

Slowly Kendai, his broad back stained in a shawl of sweat, leveled the aircraft. Now would come the even more difficult task of landing.

Saturday   10/24/13

I passed the Midtown Bookstore today and noticed a poster for a book signing with my name on it. I went inside and at a table sat the man from the subway: my Doppelganger with a beard, signing copies of a hardcover book entitled The Lost Journal. He looked up and smiled; he looked right through me, as though I wasn't even there.

Have I fabricated all this: fashioned fact from fiction? Was I living with eyes closed, misunderstanding all I saw? Maybe I have an alter ego, a second self, some other Kevin, a doppelganger that has done all this. Or perhaps he's me from an alternate universe allowed by the "Many Worlds" theory of physics.

Or perhaps. I've just imagined it.